The Elephant
And
The Stone

John L Petsco Jr.

Because we walk together
Himilce
Victoria
Gia
Zachary

Without the guidance of my teacher,
Dr. JoAnn Layford,
this book would not have been possible.

CHAPTER ONE

During one of the worst droughts in Africa in over a hundred years, lightning reached out in a long arc from the black night sky. The dry and withered grasslands quickly burst into flames.

For days the fire burned, blackening everything in its path. Whole villages disappeared, jungles turned to ash, animals perished, and scattered.

The sky was so filled with smoke that one could no longer tell night from day.

Day would fight its way into the blackness of night and smoke. The night and the smoke would extinguish the day. This battle continued for days, until after the fire had burnt everything that there was to burn. It slowly faded into the earth without even a glance back on the destruction it had caused. It was done.

In the morning the sun rose, this time without a fight. Slowly the smoke began to lift from the lands. The sky began to clear, and all that could be seen were the charred remains of what once was. An elephant appeared out of the clearing smoky haze. She was the only member of what had been a great herd. Some had run in fear, some had perished, but she alone remained. She had survived.

She knew that in this blackened land she was alone. There was nothing left for her, no companionship, no nourishment. What once was, was no more. She must leave.

From the older members of her herd, she had heard tales of great fires that had happened before and of a far off place that elephants would journey to when what was, was no more.

Without a look back, as there was nothing left to see of what once was, she started to walk.

Slowly, one foot after the other, head down, she moved forward.

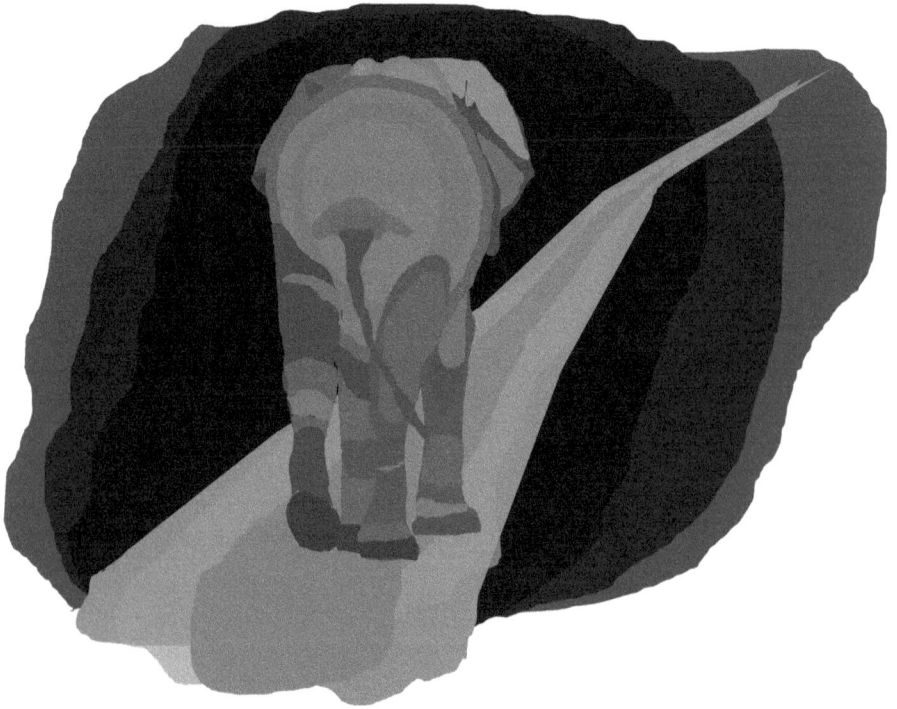

CHAPTER TWO

The Journey on her path into her future had begun. Not knowing how she was going to get there, she had decided that she would walk.

She hadn't walked very far when she came upon a small boy. Lost and in tears, he was the only survivor of what was once a village.

The elephant stopped to comfort the boy, as she knew what it was like to be alone.

"They are gone," said the boy.

"Who is gone?" said the elephant.

"My parents, and all of my family, everyone in my village they passed away," said the boy.

She gave this great thought, as elephants never think of other elephants as gone.

"They're not gone, they're just not here," said the elephant.

"What do you mean? I know they passed away in the great fire, they ARE gone!" said the boy.

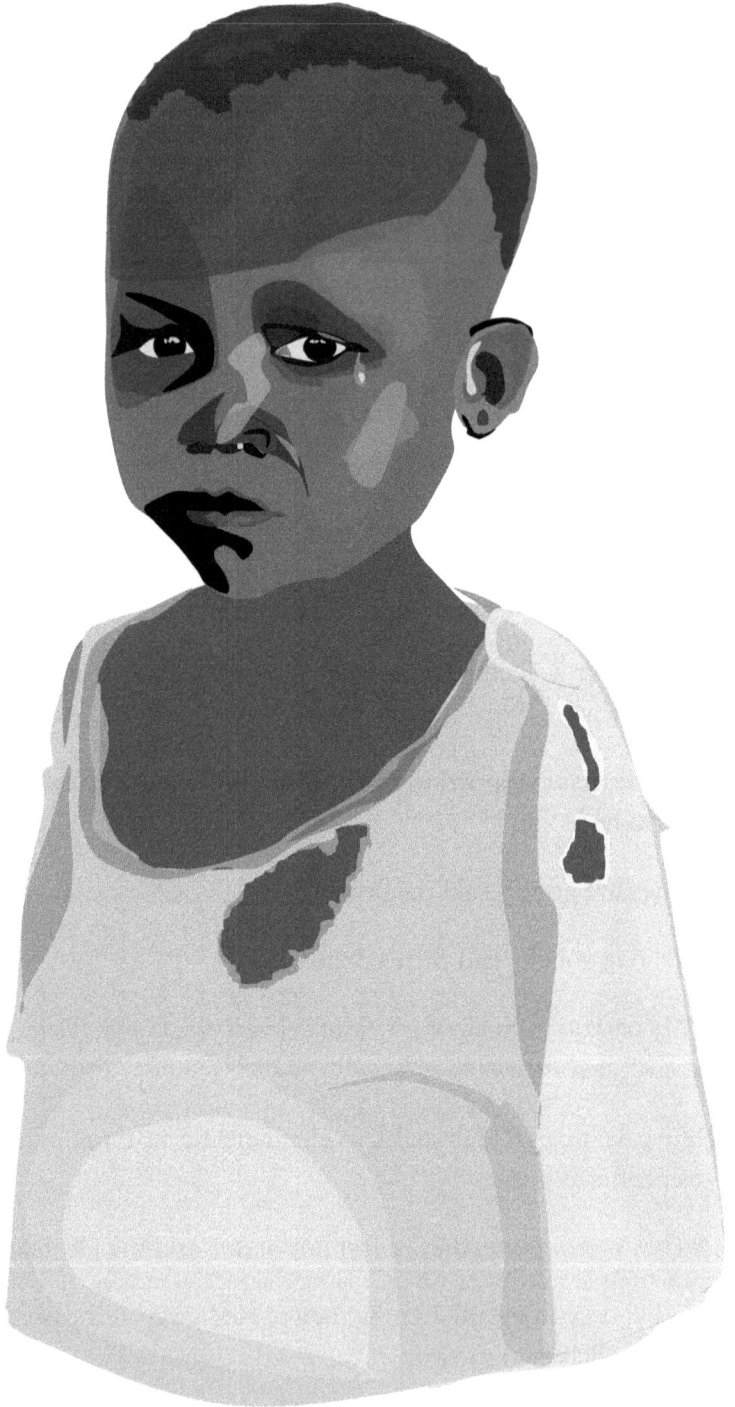

"Do you think of your parents and your family?" asked the elephant.

"Oh yes, every day!" said the boy.

"Do you love them?" asked the elephant.

"Very much!" said the boy.

"When you think of them, can you see them?" said the elephant.

The boy closed his eyes and began to think of his parents and family, how much they loved him and how much he loved them, and he could see their faces clearly as if they were standing with him!

"You are right! They are not gone, they are just not here!" said the boy.

"Those around you that you cared for and cared for you, will always be here. As elephants, we never forget any members of our herd, even those that are not here, because once we have walked, we will always walk together," said the elephant.

CHAPTER THREE

"It is time for you to leave this place, what once was, is no more. I am traveling, walk with me and I will help you on your journey to a new far off place where you will not be alone and can find the nourishment you need," said the elephant.

"Far away! I don't really know where it is I'm going, what it will be like, how difficult it will be and how I will get there," said the boy.

"As with any journey, the destination is always there. It is your desire to make the journey, to stay on the path and continue to that destination. That is the difficult part."

"Since you already know where you are, and you know where you want to go, all you have to do is make the decision to start on the path," said the elephant.

"It is so far!" said the boy.

"I have traveled thousands of miles with other elephants to visit watering holes, the only way I know how to get anywhere is to walk," said the elephant.

"But how can I walk with you? I am not an elephant," said the boy

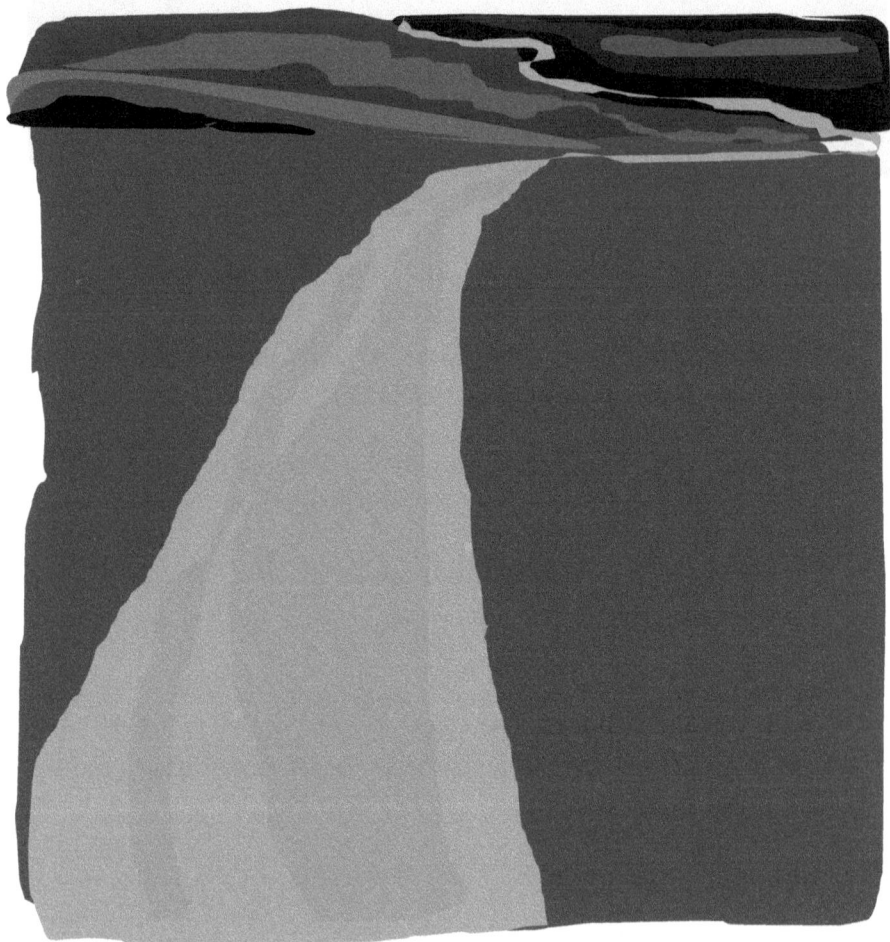

"Ever since I've been an elephant I could walk."

"And ever since you've been a boy you could walk."

"What difference does it make if you're not an elephant and I'm not a boy?"

"Since we both know how to walk, we can walk together," said the elephant.

The boy thought about this, and said, "You are right, the fact that we both can walk makes us the same."

The boy looked up and said to the elephant, "Shall we walk?"

And so the journey began, the boy and the elephant walking

Not as an elephant, or as a boy, but as travelers walking together on a single path.

Slowly, one foot after the other, heads down, they moved forward.

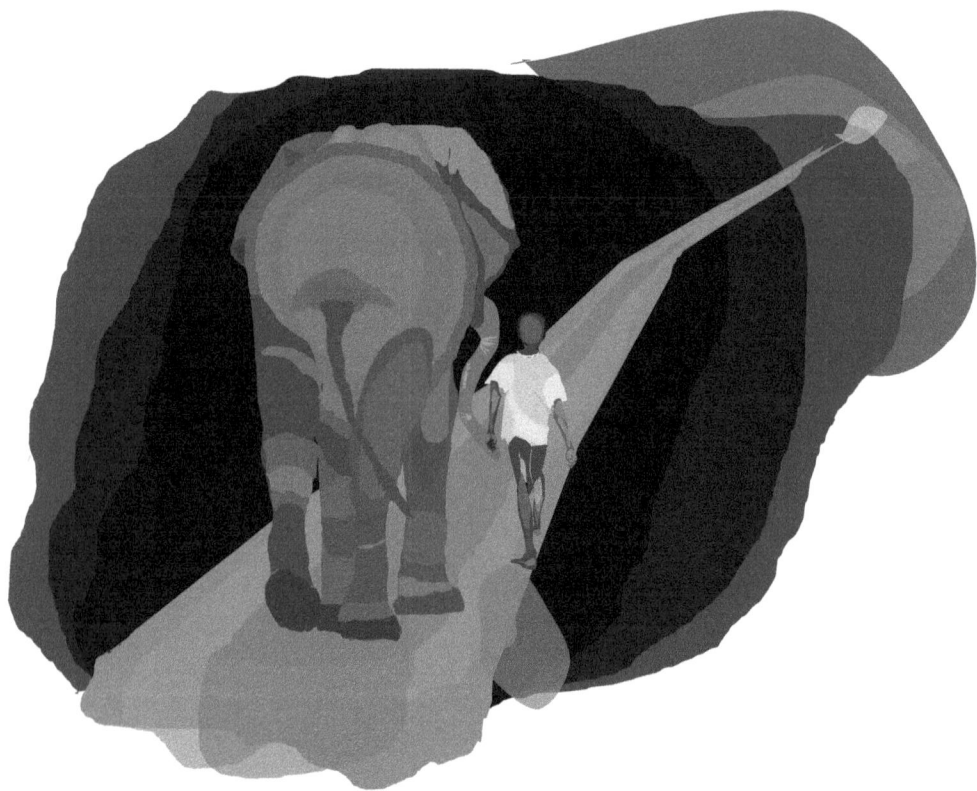

CHAPTER FOUR

"I am afraid," said the boy.

"Of what?" said the elephant.

"Of the journey, I am afraid that we might get lost, that it will be too hard," said the boy.

"You are right, it may be hard, it may be hot, and it may cold. We might even stray off the path and get lost."

"There will be rivers to cross, long walks through the jungle and days on the grasslands where time seems to stand still," said the elephant.

"So I am right to be afraid!" said the boy.

"Yes, you may be right to be afraid, but this is a journey, you cannot expect nothing to happen."

"Something always happens, every day, It is the way of life."

"It is natural to fear the unknown, but it is also a gift to understand fear. Once you understand what it is you fear, you know what it is you must overcome."

"If we stray from the path and get lost, we will find it again as long as we continue seeking the right path. The hard parts of the journey, will be equal to the good parts of the journey. We will face our fears and they will resolve themselves as we advance on our journey down the path. No one saves us from our fears but ourselves. No one can and no one may. We ourselves must walk the path," said the elephant.

The boy, afraid as he was of what might happen on the journey began to walk again.

Slowly, one foot after the other, heads down, they moved forward.

CHAPTER FIVE

"I am hungry," said the boy.

"Then we shall stop and eat," said the elephant.

"I do not have any food," said the boy.

"Nor do I. But the earth has a way of providing for those that seek nourishment," said the elephant.

"I do not see anything to eat and the fire has consumed everything," said the boy.

"The fire has consumed only that which lived upon the surface of the earth and had lost the spirit of living. What has deep roots in the spirit of life has survived," said the elephant.

"How can that be, everything that was, has been has been burned," said the boy.

"Everything? Are you burned?" asked the elephant.

"No I did not get burned by the fire, but everything, everyone I loved, everything I cherished has been burnt away," said the boy

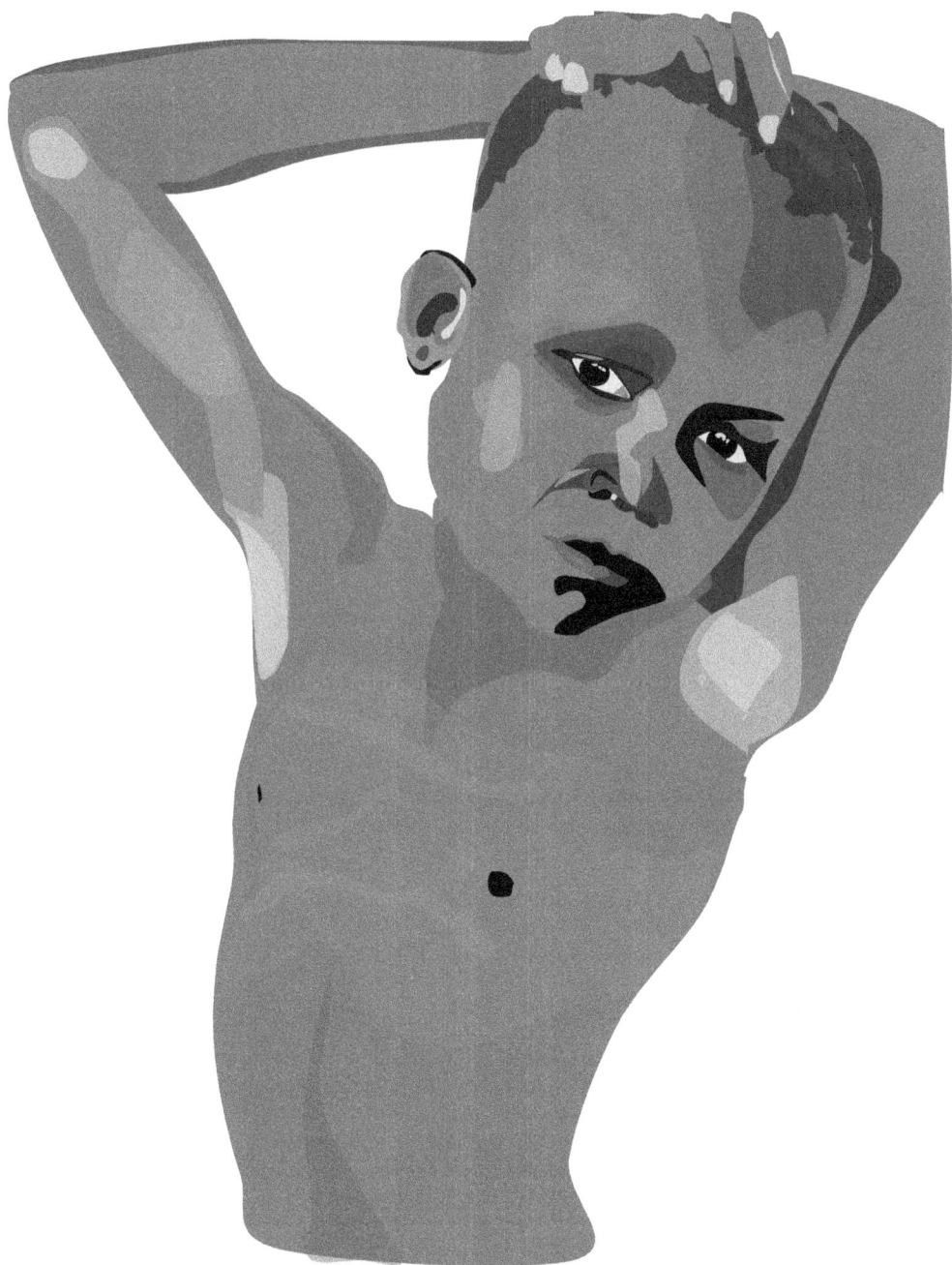

"Then not everything has been consumed by the fire. Everything you once had, you will have again Everyone you loved, you can still love. Everything you cherished, you can still cherish. All the nourishment you require, still exists, if you are willing to search for it," said the elephant.

"I am hungry, I am willing to look, but all I can see is the burnt blackness," said the boy.

"You must not simply look, but seek what you are after," said the elephant.

With that, the elephant picked up the boy and held him to the top of the nearest blackened tree.

"What is it you see?" asked the elephant.

"Three bananas!" exclaimed the boy.

"Pick two for us," said the elephant.

The boy reached into the blackened remains of the tree and picked two of the bananas. The elephant then set him gently on the ground.

"I did not see the bananas from where I am standing," said the boy.

*"That is because you were only looking, and not seeking.
In life to find what you require, you must look beyond what is.
What you require could be above or below or even behind you.
Many starve in this world because they simply look and do not seek out the nourishment they require,"* said the elephant.

"But I did look and I did not see them," said the boy.

"What did you search with?" asked the elephant.

"Why of course with my eyes. What else could I search with?" said the boy.

"When you are searching for something you require in life you need look with more than your eyes," said the elephant.

"What else can I look with beside my eyes?" asked the boy.

"If you were to close your eyes, can you tell that the sun is shining?" asked the elephant.

"Why of course," said the boy.

"How can you tell?" asked the elephant.

"I can feel it, I can sense it, it makes me warm," said the boy.

"Is the sun something you seek every day?" asked the elephant.

"No, it's always been there and always will be," said the boy.

The elephant nodded;

"If you are open to what it is you are searching for, you do not need your eyes to see. Just as you do not need your eyes to see the sun, you do not need them to see the nourishment you seek. Had you not looked only with your eyes but also with your heart and your mind, you would have climbed the tree and above the blackened existence you would have found the nourishment you seek," said the elephant.

The boy thought about all the times he had gone searching for something but went only looking.

"I have missed so much along this journey," said the boy.

"Well, know that you know how to see; shall we walk?" said the elephant.

And they did, slowly. One foot after the other, heads down, they moved forward.

CHAPTER SIX

"Why did you have me take only two bananas when we could have taken all three?" asked the boy.

"There are only two of us that need to eat, not three," said the elephant.

"But we could have eaten the third one later," said the boy.

"The third one was left there to be shared," said the elephant.

"But with whom? There are only two of us on this journey; we are alone!" said the boy.

"Alone? There may be only two of us walking, an elephant and a boy, but this journey consists of more than just you and me," said the elephant.

"How can that be, we are the only ones," said the boy.

"On this path we also travel with;
The memories of the lands as they once were,
The memories of your life as it was,
The love of your family,
The love of my herd,
The fears and dreams of what life will be,

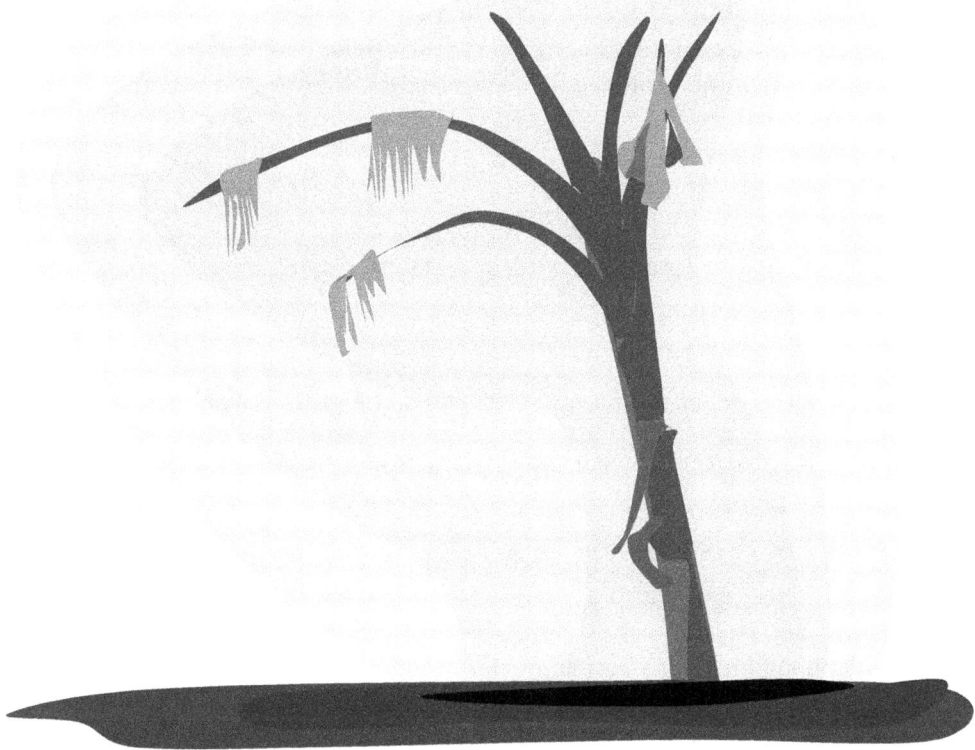

What is left of the lands as they are now,
The tree that provided the nourishment we needed,
The path of the journey itself,
The footprints of those that have journeyed before us,
And the hope of others that might find our path and follow it,
We are not alone."

"By leaving the last banana, we have shared the gift of life.
From that single remaining banana;
A traveler on this path seeking nourishment will leave the seeds behind,
The seeds will seek nourishment from the scorched earth,
The rains, when they come, will help the seeds to grow and become trees,
The trees will become a jungle again,
And the animals will return,
And what is now, will become what was, again,
We have shared with many," said the elephant.

The boy thought about this, and after awhile he said to the elephant,

"On this journey, all I've thought about is all I've lost, all that is gone and how I have nothing left, but to walk. Now I can see that I have so much to give, that I have more than I'll ever require as long as I am on the path and continue to walk."

The elephant smiled, as best an elephant can do.

"Shall we walk?" asked the elephant.

And they did, slowly. One foot after the other, heads down, they moved forward.

CHAPTER SEVEN

For days they walked, the boy as just a boy and the elephant as just an elephant.

With each step the blackness of the scorched earth lessened and the brightness of the living earth grew.

"We are lost," said the boy.

"How can you tell?" asked the elephant.

"Well we have been walking for days and we haven't arrived yet," said the boy.

"Where is it, that we haven't arrived yet?" asked the elephant.

"Our destination!" exclaimed the boy.

"We must be lost, as we seem to be wandering around on this path through the jungle, and it does not seem to be taking us anywhere," said the boy.

"All that wander, are not lost. The path is simply a path, no more no less, it just is," said the elephant.

"How can that be? We are following the path, we did not make it," said the boy.

"The path did not create itself; it simply exists as a memory of those that have journeyed before us. The path is simply there to guide us on our journey. The path doesn't care where it begins, how long it is, whether it is difficult, whether it even ends, or if it is even the right path. When we are on the path, it is our path and ours alone, our steps leave behind the past and take us forward into the future.

We are not lost, you simply are not sure of where we are.

If you believe that we are lost, then we will be lost, so do not think of us as lost, but as a boy and an elephant, walking on a path into what will be," said the elephant.

"Now look behind you and then look in front of you, which direction would you choose? The journey back into the blackened past?, or into the brightness of the future?" asked the elephant.

The boy turned and looked at where they had walked, and saw that they were not lost, but had already journeyed so far from their past, that everything no longer looked like it once was.

Turning toward the future, the boy asked of the elephant, "Shall we walk?"

Together, they smiled as best as a boy could and as best as an elephant could, and they began to walk as two travelers on the same path.

And they did, slowly. One foot after the other, heads down, they moved forward.

CHAPTER EIGHT

During the day they walked along the path, the boy and the elephant side by side. At night the elephant would lay down and the boy would curl up next to the elephant, tuck himself under her large ear, and wrap his arms around her neck.

His dreams would start as memories of what once was, but would always end in visions of what will be. He was losing his fear of the path and of what lay ahead. His mind and heart had opened, now no longer just a boy, but student of the journey.

The living earth grew greener with each step, the grasslands appeared and gave way to the jungle. The blackness they had left behind was no longer visible on their path.

Day after day they walked, following the path, not questioning it, but simply following it, as it did not question their reasons for walking on it. Slowly, the path began to rise up through the jungle leading them to the base of a large mountain.

"How will we ever climb that? It is too high!" said the boy.

"Slowly," said the elephant.

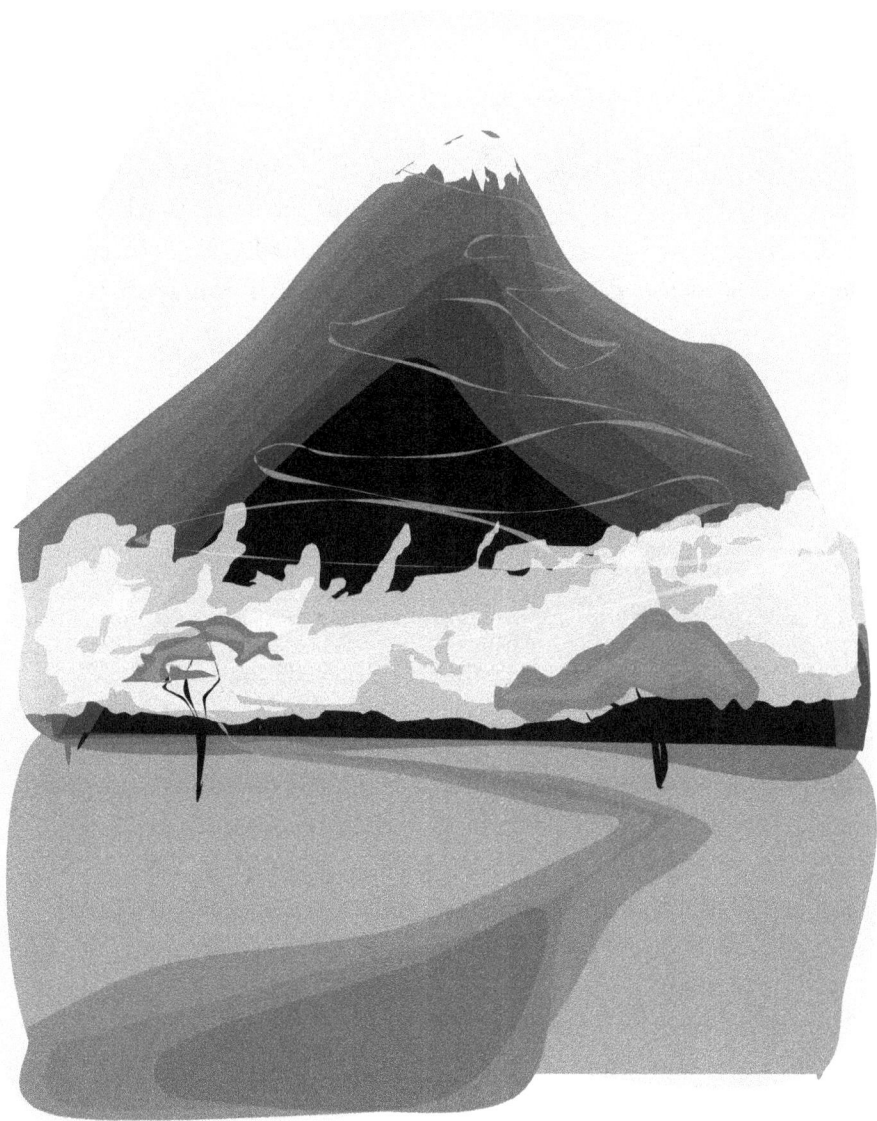

"There must be a way around it!" exclaimed the boy.

"No. Our path leads to the mountain, we must climb," said the elephant.

"The path is too long and steep, it will take a long time to get to the top," said the boy.

"Yes it will, the path simply leads us from what once was to what will be. *Remember the path is just a memory of those that had journeyed before us; it is not a fault of the path that we must climb this mountain. We will not be the first ones to make this journey over this mountain. You can choose to see the mountain as an obstacle on your path, or you can choose to see it as an opportunity to climb. As an elephant who has walked many paths, I have found that a path with no obstacles usually doesn't lead anywhere. It is your choice to make,*" said the elephant.

The boy stood and looked at the top of the mountain, wondering if he had the will to make it to the top.

"I don't know if I can make it to the top," said the boy.

"Nor do I. But we have learned that a boy and an elephant can walk together, side by side. *We shall walk, taking each step for what it is, simply a step forward. We shall not look down to see where we have walked from for that is in the past, nor shall we look up to see how far we have to go, for that is in the future, we shall look at the path as it is where we are now and every step forward brings us closer to the top,*" said the elephant.

The boy freeing himself of his fears, turned to the elephant and said;

"Shall we walk?"

And they did, slowly. One foot after the other, heads down, they moved forward.

CHAPTER NINE

Days turned into weeks. The boy, no longer just a boy and the elephant still just an elephant climbed. Every step, took them higher, closer to the top. The two travelers walked on a path together.

"We have made it," said the elephant.

The boy looked up from the path to see that they had indeed reached the top of what had once seemed impossible.

"The mountain does not seem so big now," said the boy.

"Once you have made the climb, it is hard to see the mountain from the top," said the elephant.

"I was so sure that this path that lead us to this mountain was the wrong one, and that there must have be an easier path to follow," said the boy.

"Look all around you," said the elephant.

The boy, standing on top of the mountain looking with more than just his eyes, could see many paths, leading in many directions, going many places.

"There is more than one path!" exclaimed the boy.

"Yes, there are many paths to travel," said the elephant.

"Which way do we go?" asked the boy.

"We shall walk the path we are on, until the path is no more, until a new path appears. Each path we travel will always lead us to a new path,"

"How will we know if it is the right path?" asked the boy.

"We will not know until we have begun to walk on it."

"Shall we walk?" said the elephant.

And they did, slowly. One foot after the other, heads down, they moved forward.

CHAPTER TEN

"Why did we survive when the fire burned so many?" asked the boy.

"It is the will of the earth," said the elephant.

"The will of the earth? I do not understand," said the boy.

"There are things that will happen along the journey on the path, which will have no explanation, no reason for being, and no reason to try and understand," said the elephant.

"There must be a reason," said the boy.

"The earth is a living thing just as you a boy and I an elephant live. It breathes just as we breathe and walks around the sun, on its simple path. The earth lives in harmony with itself. It balances between what is and what will be. The fire was simply one of the earth's ways of rebalancing. The amount of what is that was lost, has made room for what will be," said the elephant.

"Then why did we survive?" asked the boy.

"Just as the banana leaves behind its seeds to start a forest, the fire left us, a boy and an elephant, behind so that the memory of what was, will not be forgotten. It was the will of the earth that we should survive. That this journey, of you and me, on a single path could begin. You a boy, and I, an elephant shall carry the memories of our journey and of what once was. We, after having learned to be students of this path can teach to others, what they can learn along their path," said the elephant.

"I have never thought of myself as a student or as a teacher. But as we walk, I have come to see that there is so much to learn, and learning must be shared, so I must teach," said the boy.

"And you shall," said the elephant.

"Shall we walk?" asked the boy.

And they did, slowly. One foot after the other, heads down, they moved forward.

CHAPTER ELEVEN

"I am free," said the boy.

"Free of what?" asked the elephant.

"Everything."

"Everything that was, everything that is, and everything that will be. We have been walking for months on the path, a simple stretch of dirt worn through the jungle and grasslands. I've been following this path believing this was the only path to my destination. I believed that path created by the journeys of others must be the only path," said the boy.

"If this is not your path, then where is it?" asked the elephant.

"It is a path that not yet has been created. Only by walking will I create my path. There is no path that exists for all, each path is different. The path we have been walking for months has only been a small part of my journey, a greater path for me waits. I have become free from the burden of my thoughts, free from the memories of what was, free from what is, free from what I thought I must be, free from the fear of what will be. I am free to walk," said the boy.

 The boy reached out and wrapped his arms around the elephant's trunk, placed his forehead against the elephants, and said, "I am free to walk with you my friend, an elephant. Shall we walk," asked the boy?

And they did, slowly. One foot after the other, heads down, they moved forward.

CHAPTER TWELVE

The jungle began to recede and give way to the grasslands, leading them to a small island of trees which divided the path.

The elephant stopped walking.

"It is time," said the elephant.

"Time for what?" said the boy.

"It is time for each of us to continue on our own path. I must walk on my own path as an elephant, and you on your own path as a boy," said the elephant.

"I do not want to walk alone; I want to continue to walk with you," said the boy.

"Ever since I was an elephant, I could walk. And ever since you've been a boy you, could walk. Together we have walked as the same, side by side. Now we will continue to walk, as a boy and as an elephant, only on different paths," said the elephant.

"I do not want to be alone!" cried the boy.

"Think about all you've learned as we've walked, are you ever alone? I care for you and you care for me, I will not be gone, just not there with you." said the elephant.

The boy put his head down in sadness. He knew in his heart that this day was to come, and now it had.

The elephant wrapped her trunk gently around the boy as only a mother elephant could and hugged the boy.

"I will miss you and hope I never forget you, you have taught me so much," said the boy.

"You have learned, because you were willing to learn. You set your mind and your heart free from all that you had learned before and allowed new light to reach into you and shine on the things you had been unable to see before," said the elephant.

A single tear fell from the elephant's eye and landed on the path. It washed away the dust revealing a single small stone.

The elephant picked it up and gave it to the boy.

"Here is something for you to remember me by, it is just a small stone, of little value, but the weight of it in your pocket will remind you of our journey together, the boy and an elephant that simply walked, because they could, on the same path," said the elephant.

The boy put the stone in his pocket, and felt the weight of it.

"I shall always carry this stone with me," said the boy

The elephant released the boy from her hug and with a gentle push guided him towards the path that would continue his journey to his destination.

"It is time," said the elephant.

"It is time," said the boy.

With a simple wave of goodbye, the boy began to walk, down the path that he must take. It was his path alone.

The elephant watched as the boy walked into the future on his path.

Slowly, one foot after the other, head down, he moved forward.

CHAPTER THIRTEEN

Once the elephant could no longer see the boy, she began to walk. Slowly, one foot after the other, head down, she moved forward.

Her path led her deep into a jungle that no fire had ever blackened, that no man had ever set foot on, and where the land that is would never become the land that was.

She had come home, to the home of her ancestors, where elephants go to rest after their long journey is complete.

She lay down among her brothers, her sisters and other members of her family. She had arrived at her destination.

The elephant smiled, as best an elephant can do and walked through the memories of her life. She could only see the good memories of her journey on her path. Scars had long since healed and faded over any injuries she had suffered along the way.

She thought of the boy and how they had walked.
Surrounded by the love of her ancestors she went to sleep for the last time.

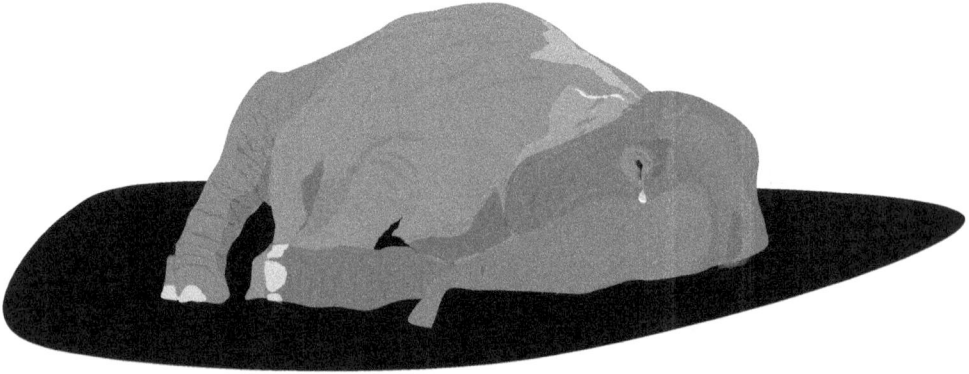

The End

I have never written a book before. This book chose me.

The elephant in the story came to me in a reoccurring dream. In my dreams, we would walk together on a path. Sometimes the path took me back into my past as a boy, and sometimes it took me into my future as a man.

I began seeing news reports on how elephants were being poisoned at their watering holes simply to get a few tusks. A whole herd, forty elephants, killed. It broke my heart.

Every night when I went to bed, the thoughts would turn into dreams, and in the morning dreams would turn into words and pictures.

It is estimated at the current rate of these mass killings that in TWELVE YEARS, there will be NO African elephants left in the wild.

A portion of the proceeds of this book will be donated to www.biglife.org   Please visit there site to learn about the wonderful things they are doing to help save the elephants and other animals.

John L Petsco Jr.

Namaste

ABOUT THE AUTHOR

John L Petsco Jr. is a builder, designer, painter,
chef, wine enthusiast, and avid skier.
Currently residing in Port Jefferson Station, NY
with his wife Himilce.
They share their property with two pot bellied pigs,
Oscar and Olivia, and Maycee, their Nubian goat.

www.ingramcontent.com/pod-product-compliance
Lightning Source LLC
Chambersburg PA
CBHW071643050426
42443CB00026B/945